If lost please return to

~~~~~~~~~~~~~~~~~~

~~~~~~~~~~~~~~~~~~

This book is dedicated to Older people and their knees.

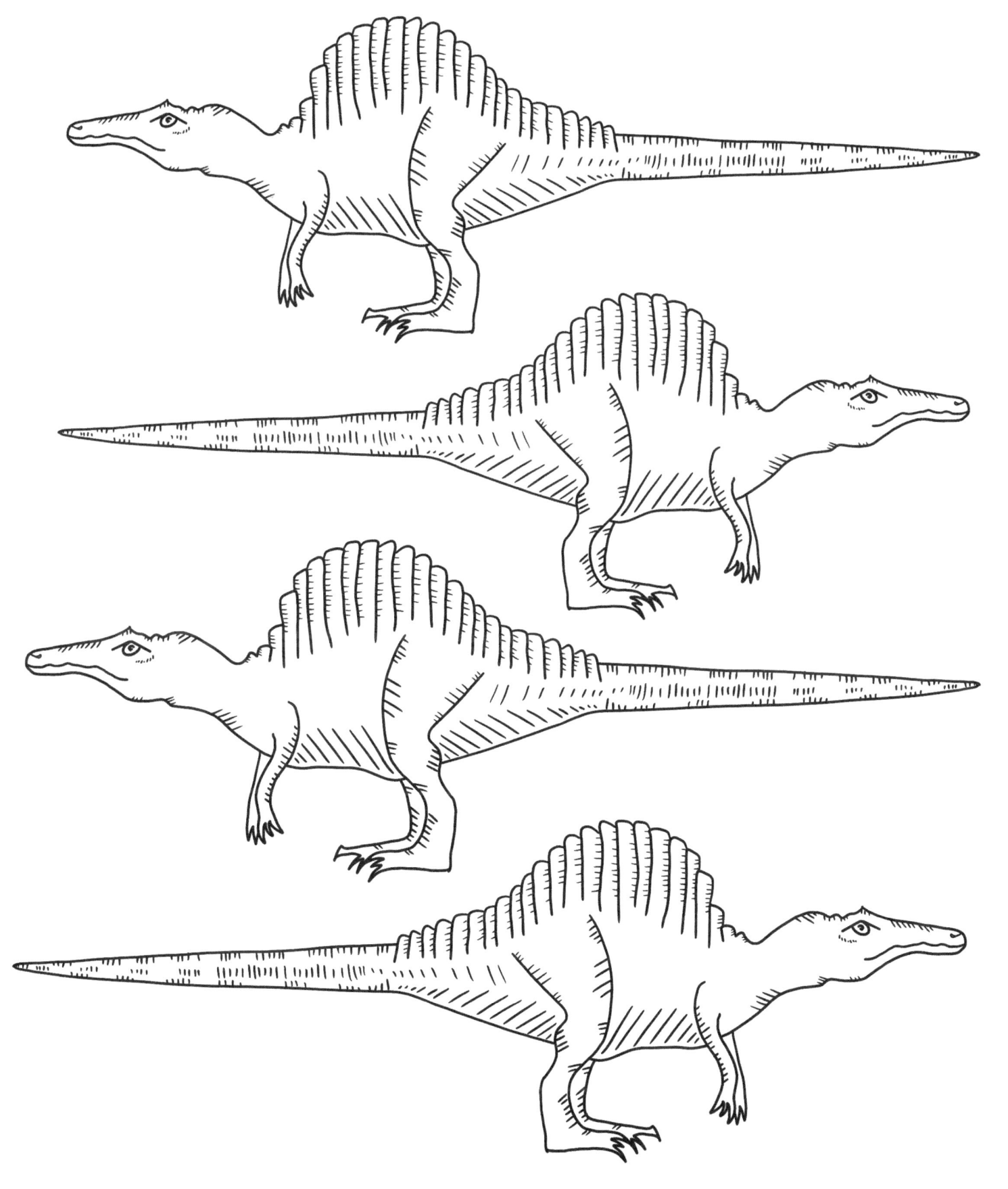

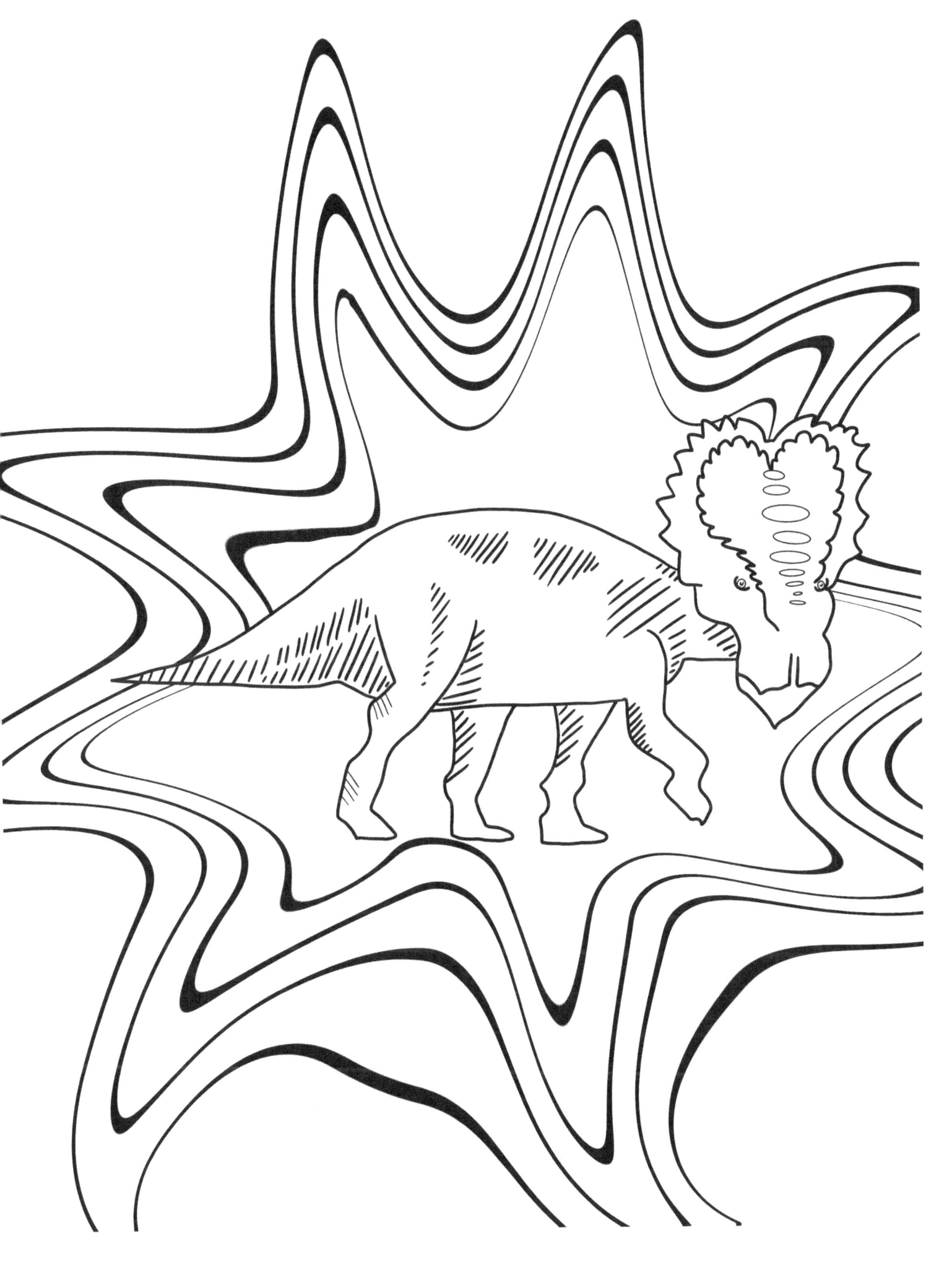

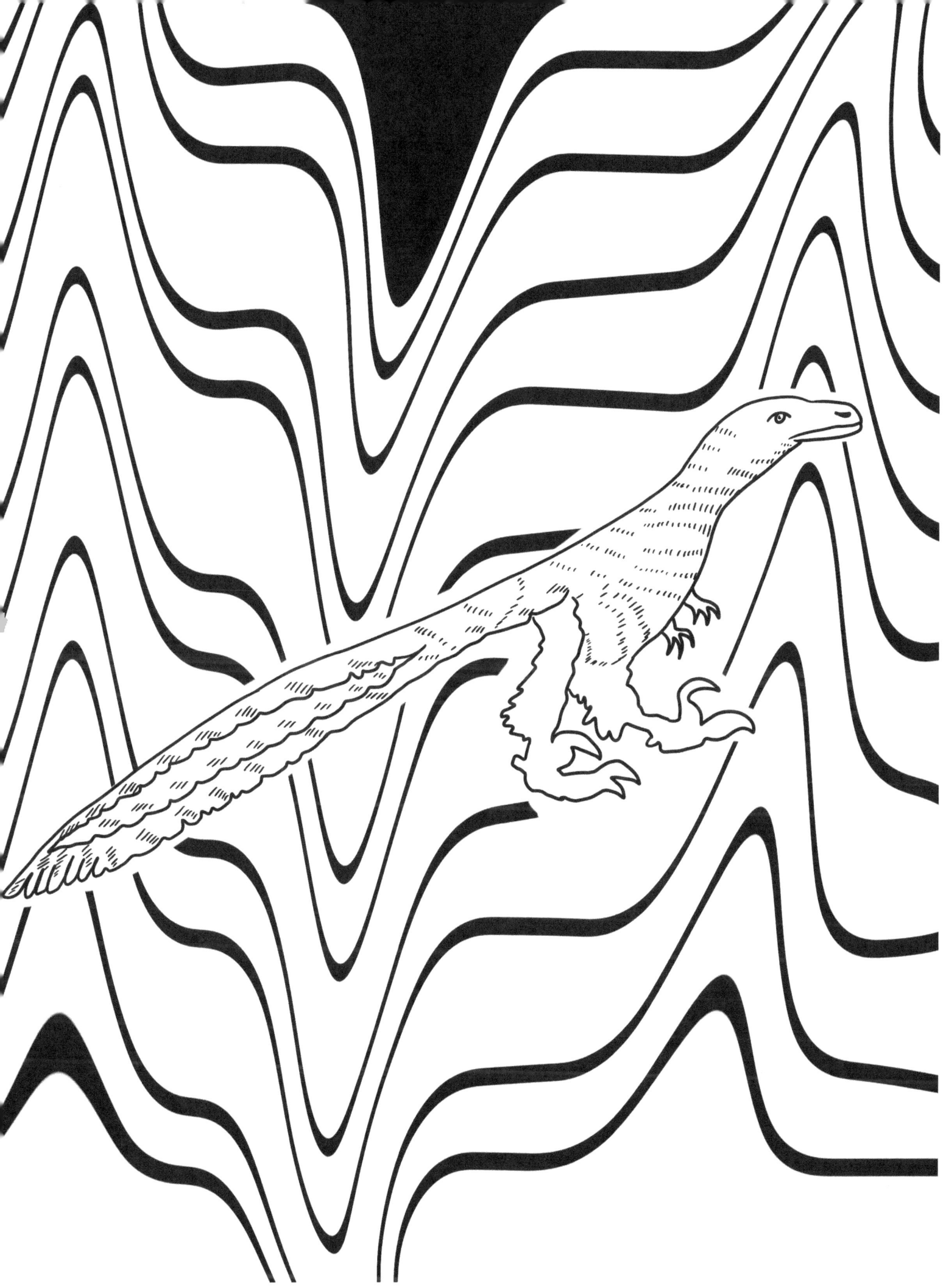

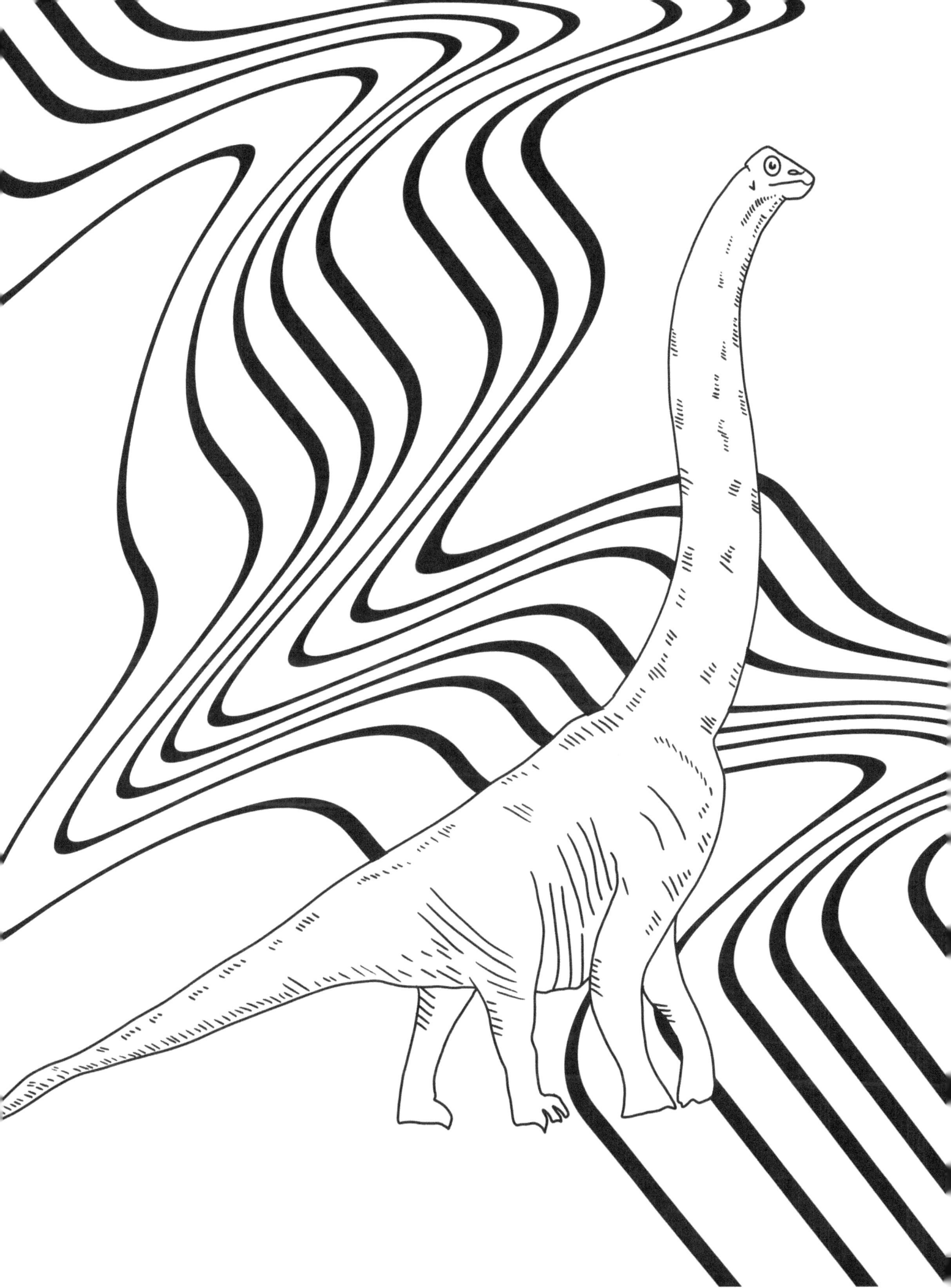

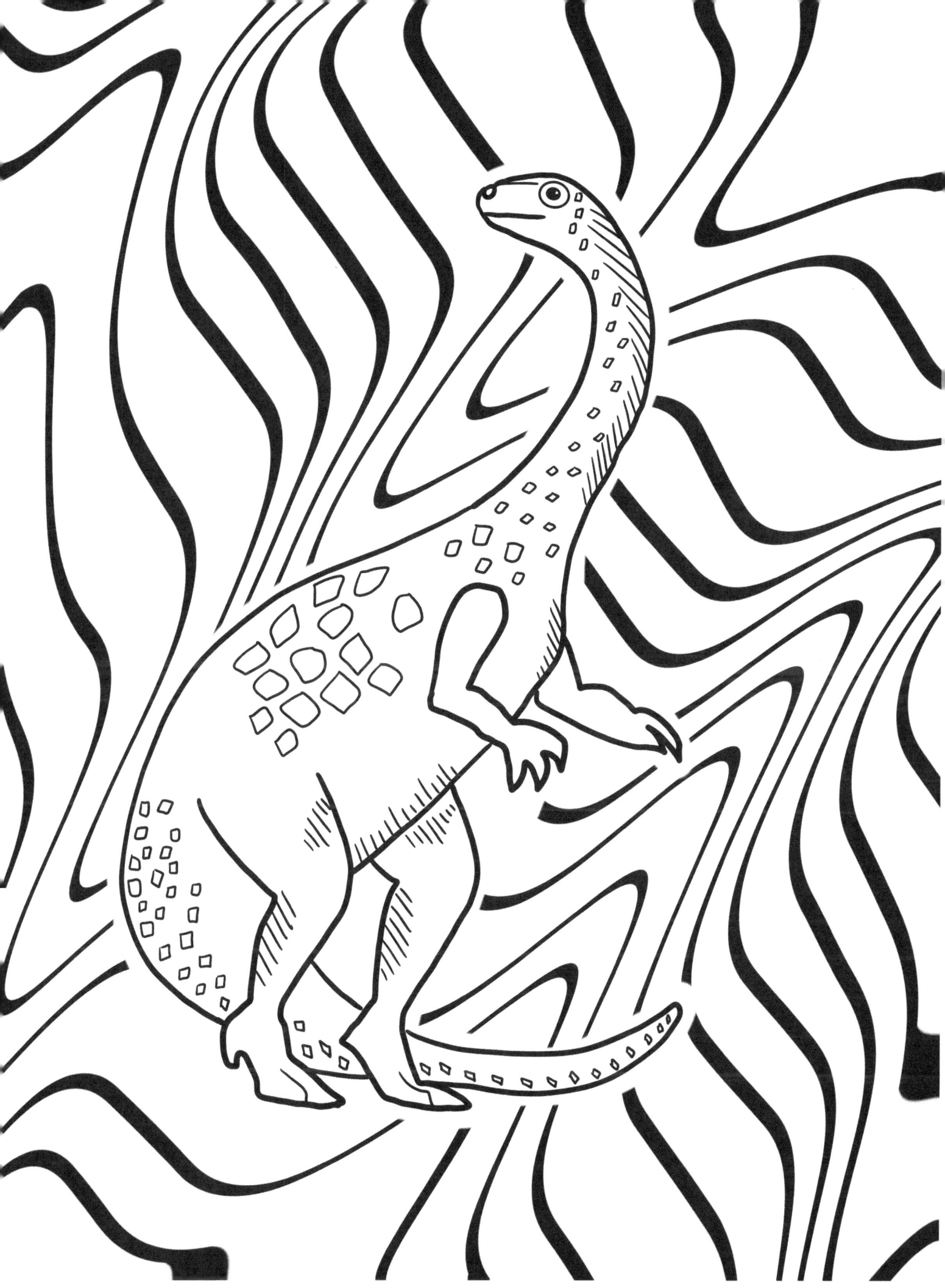

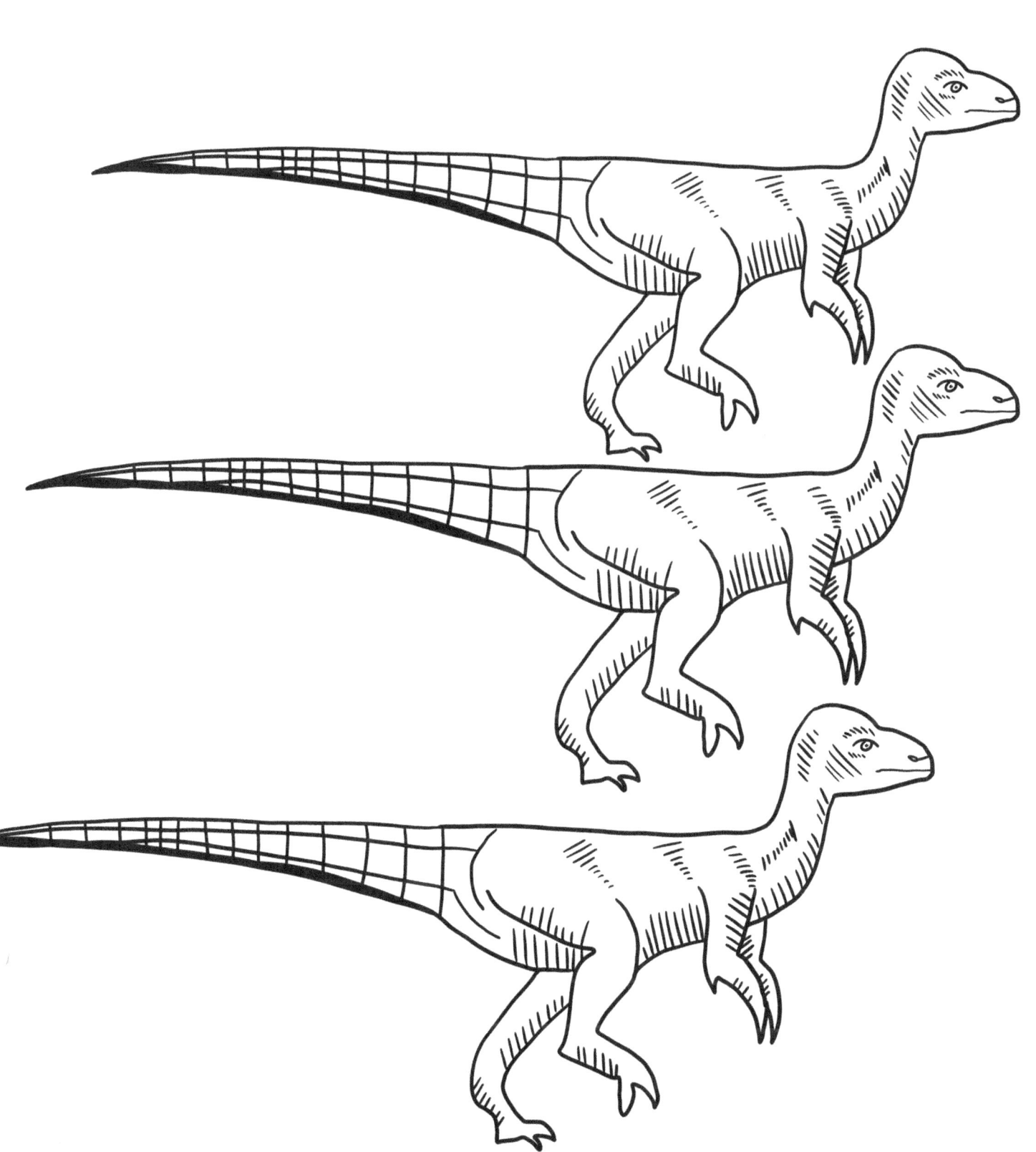

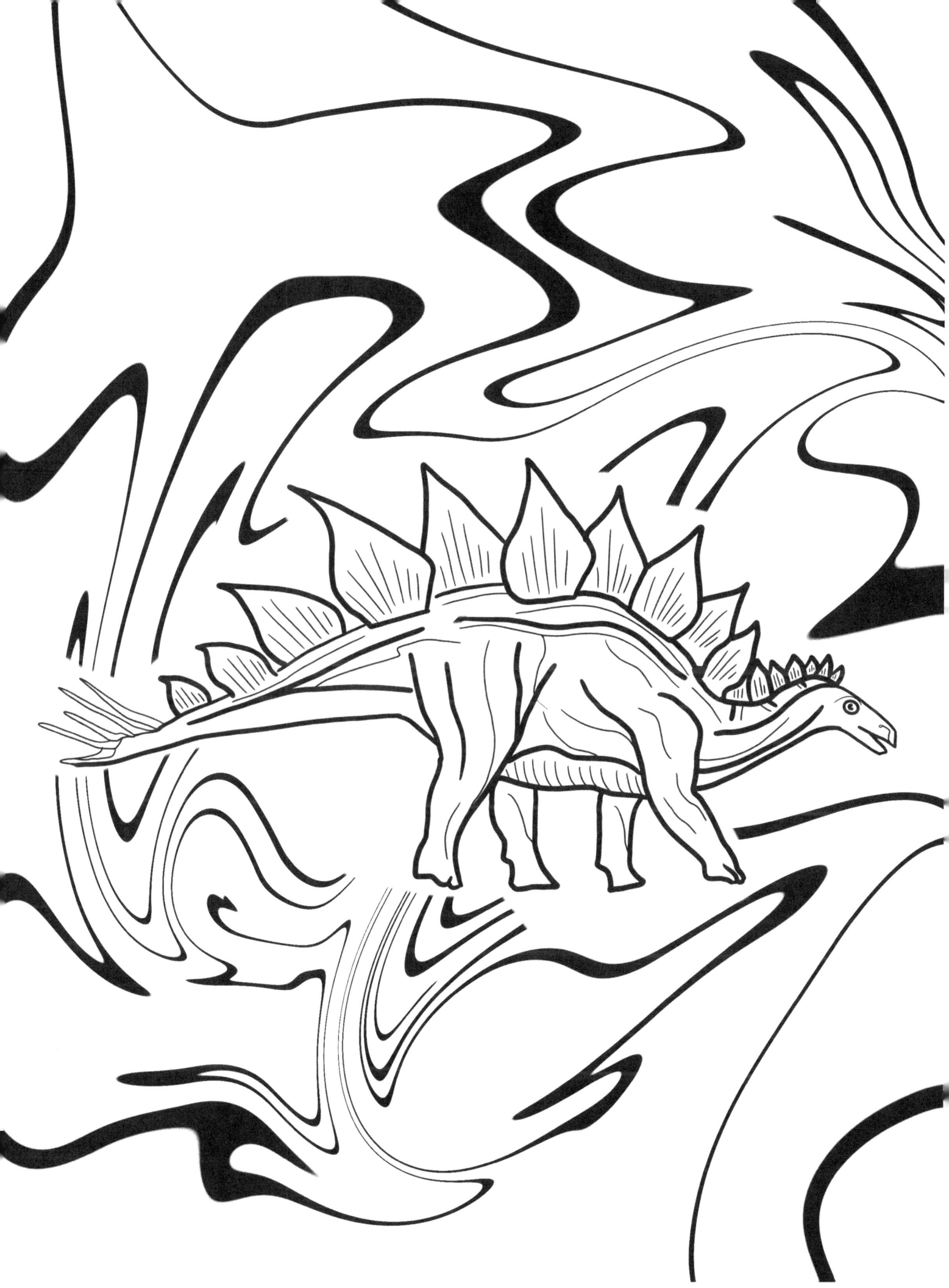

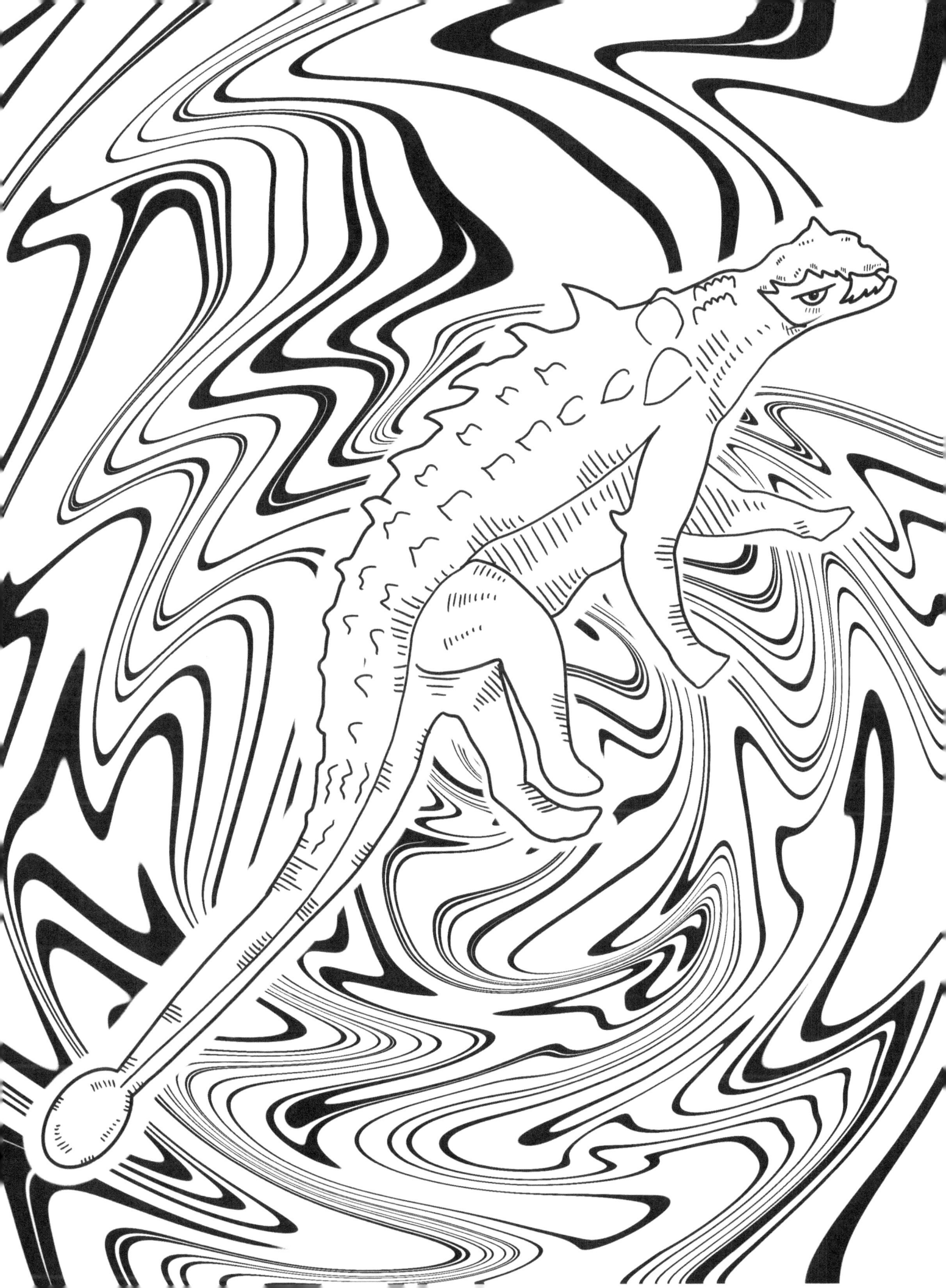

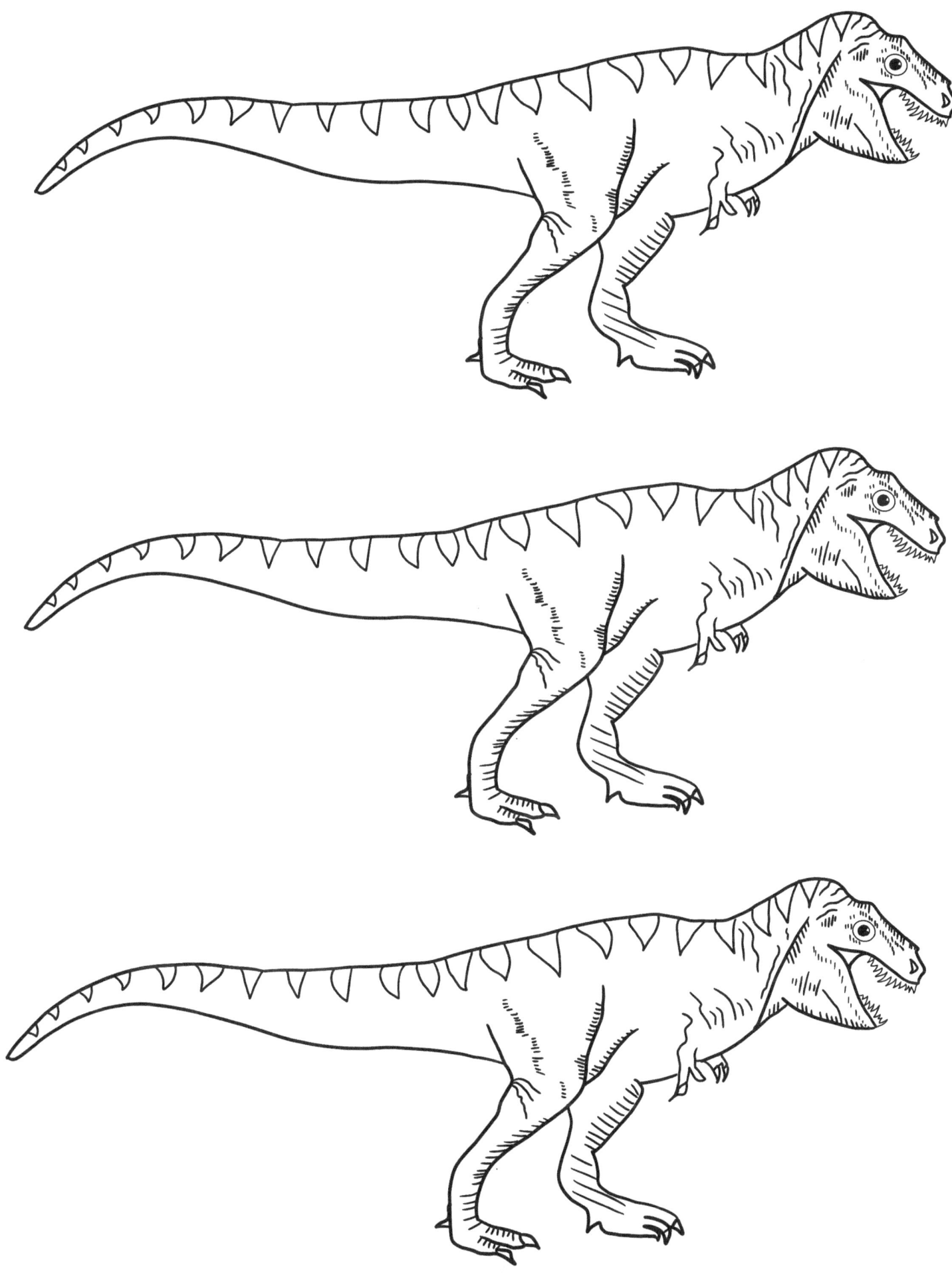

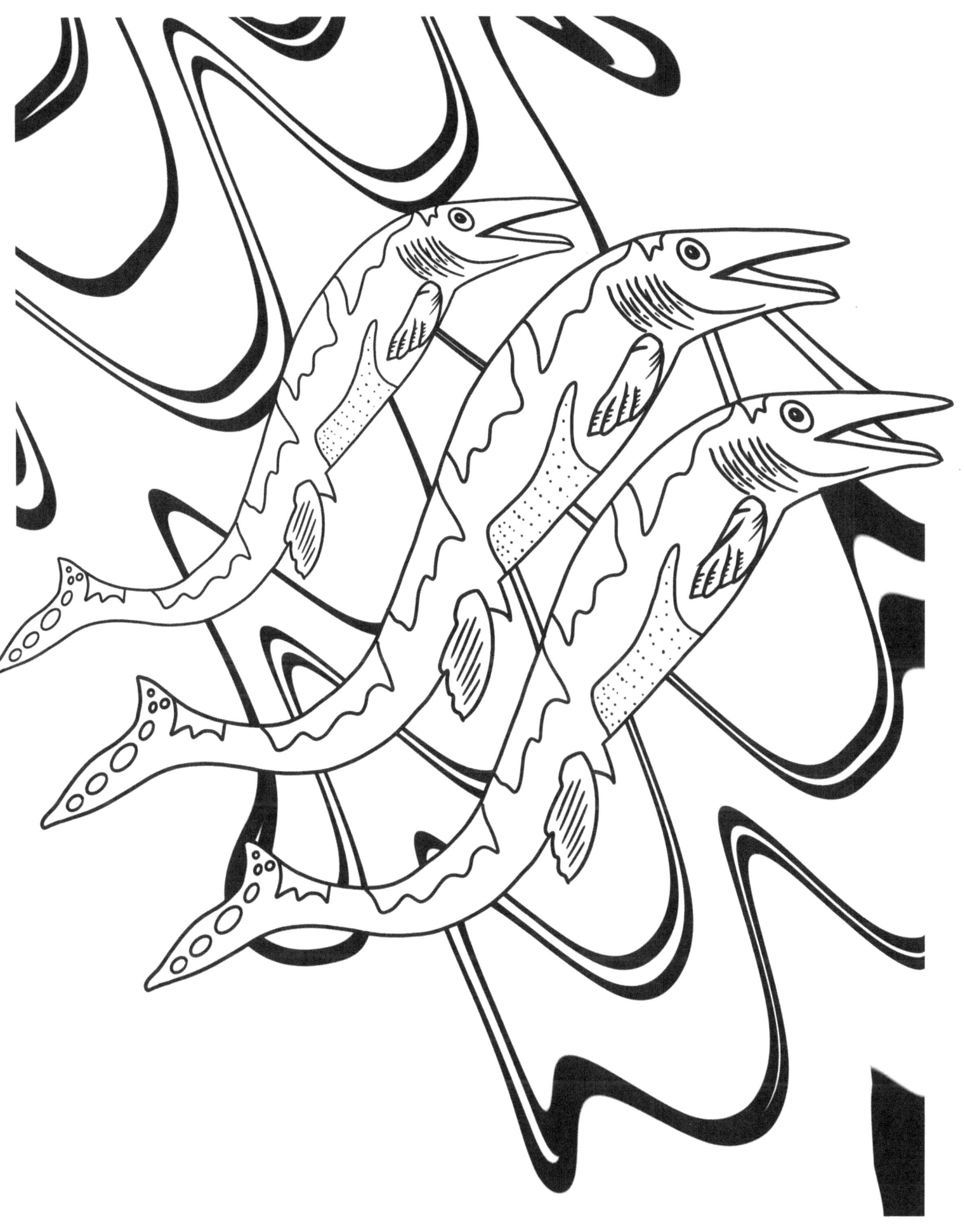

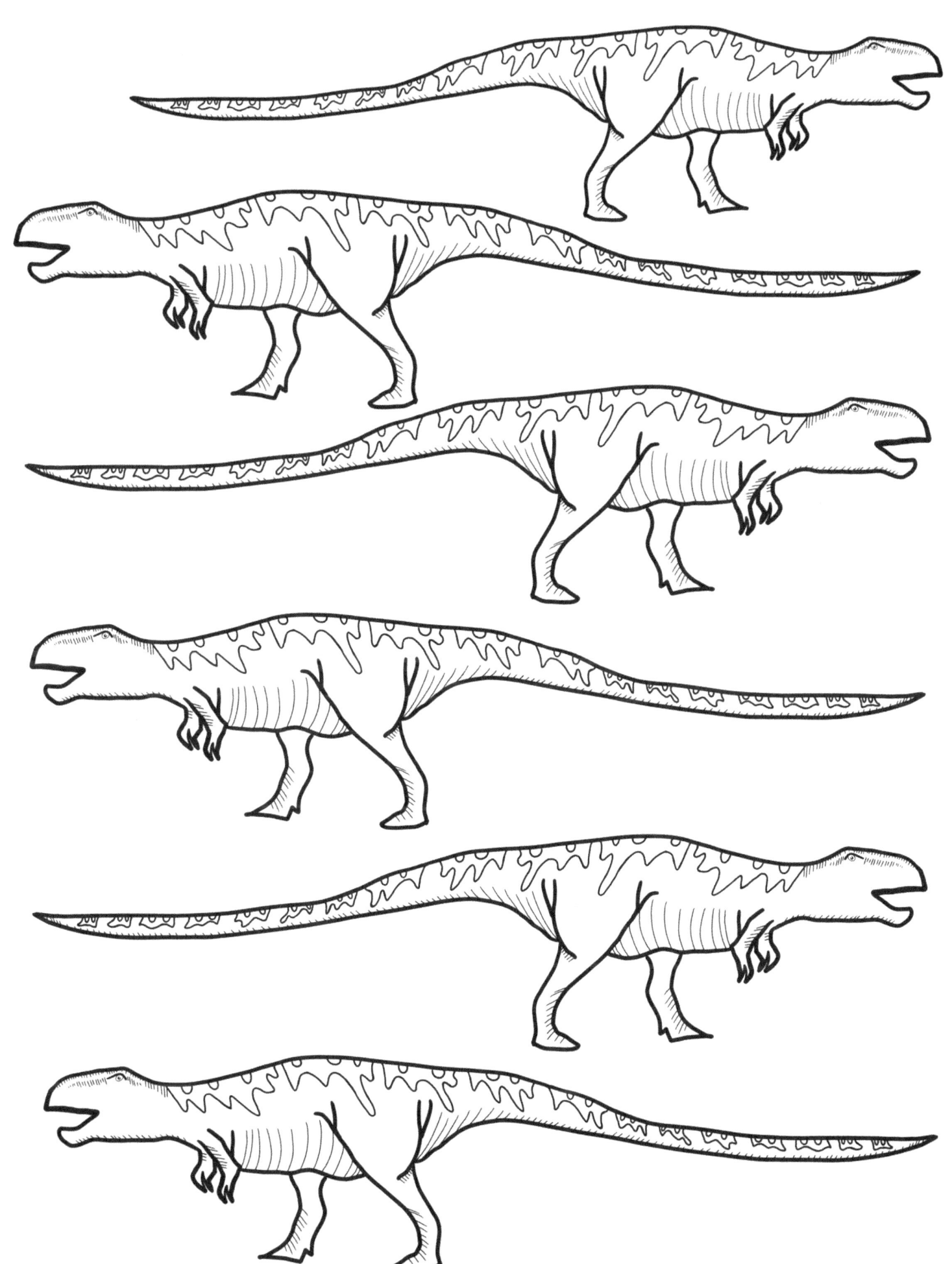

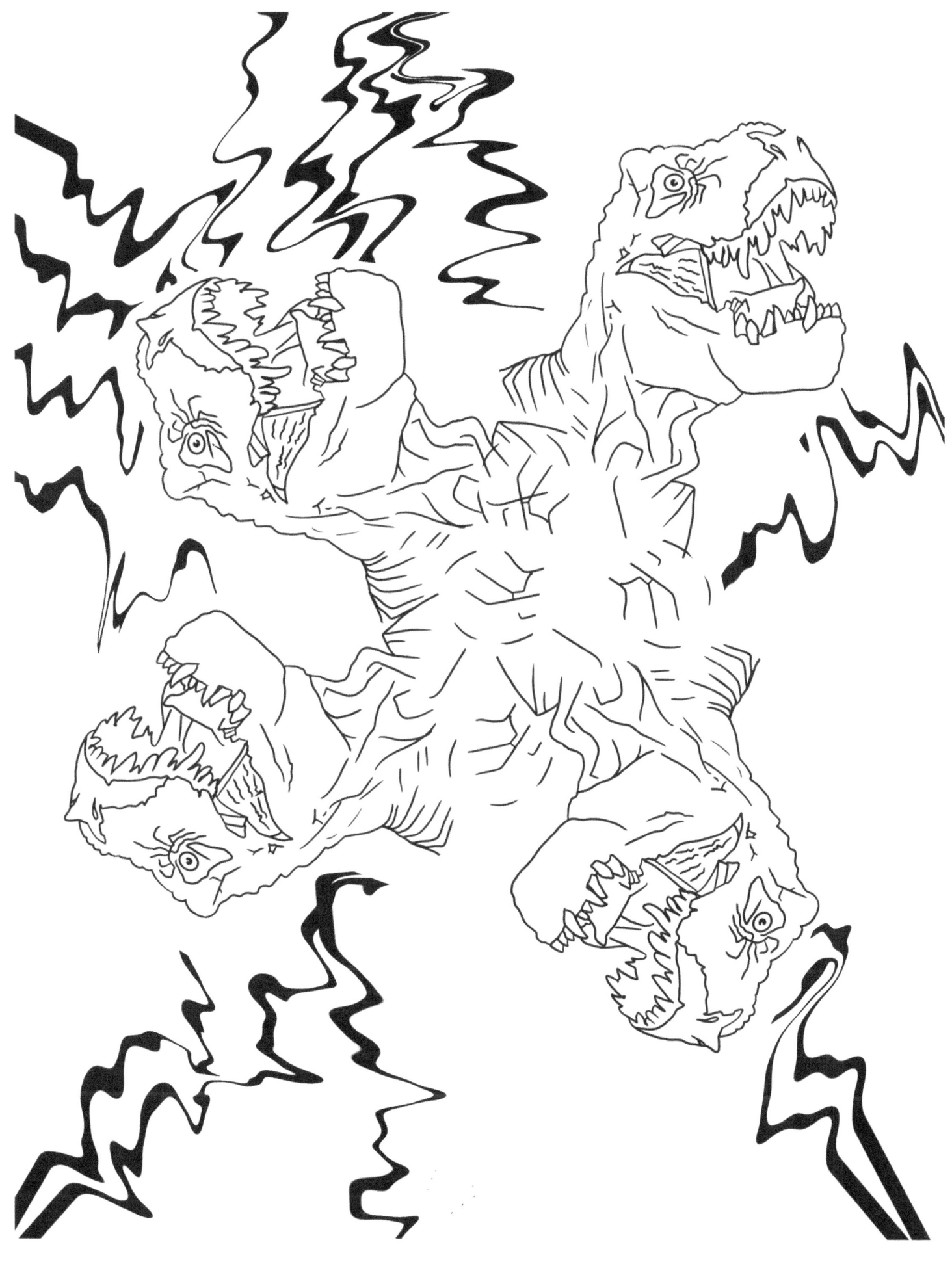

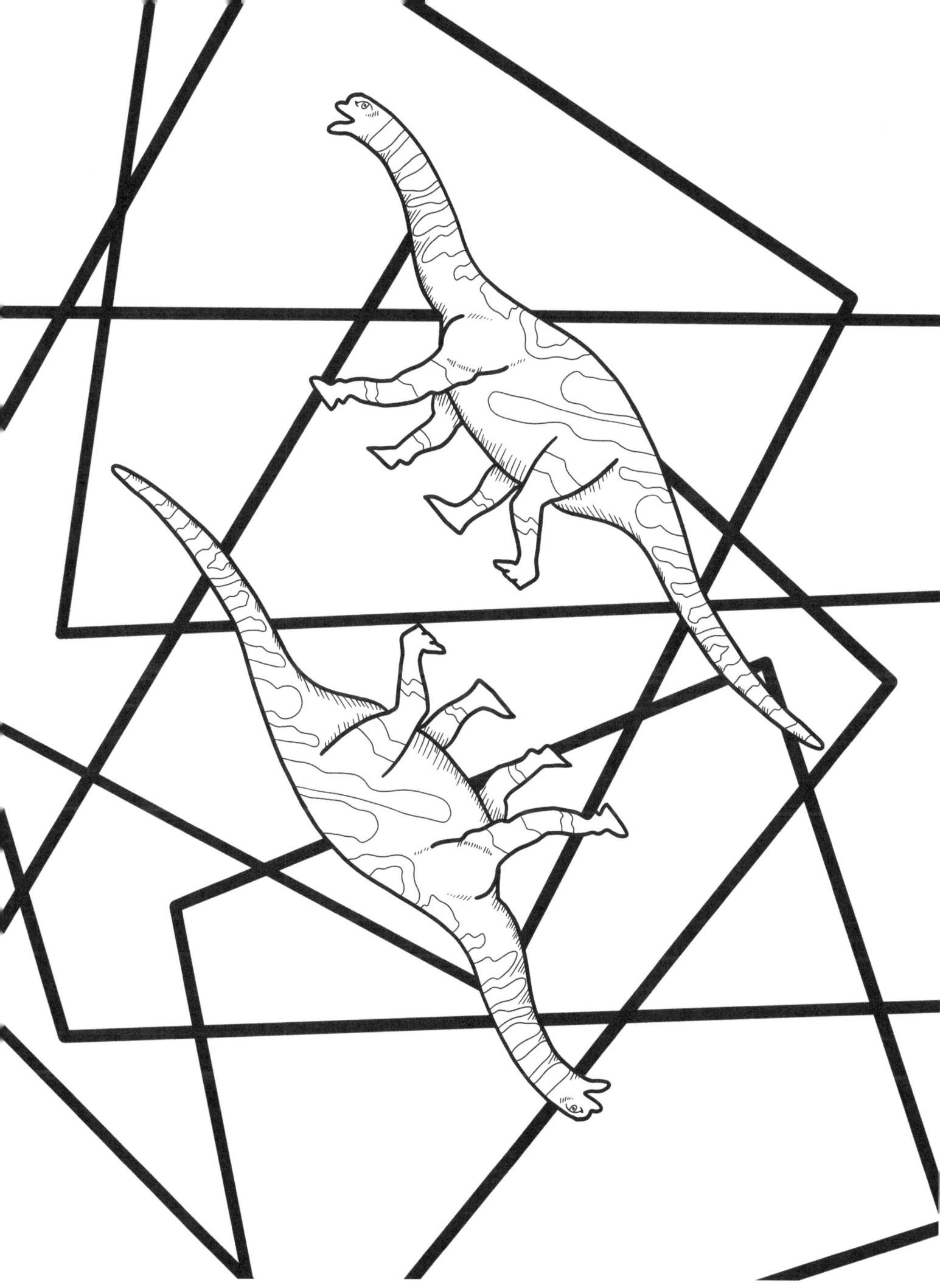

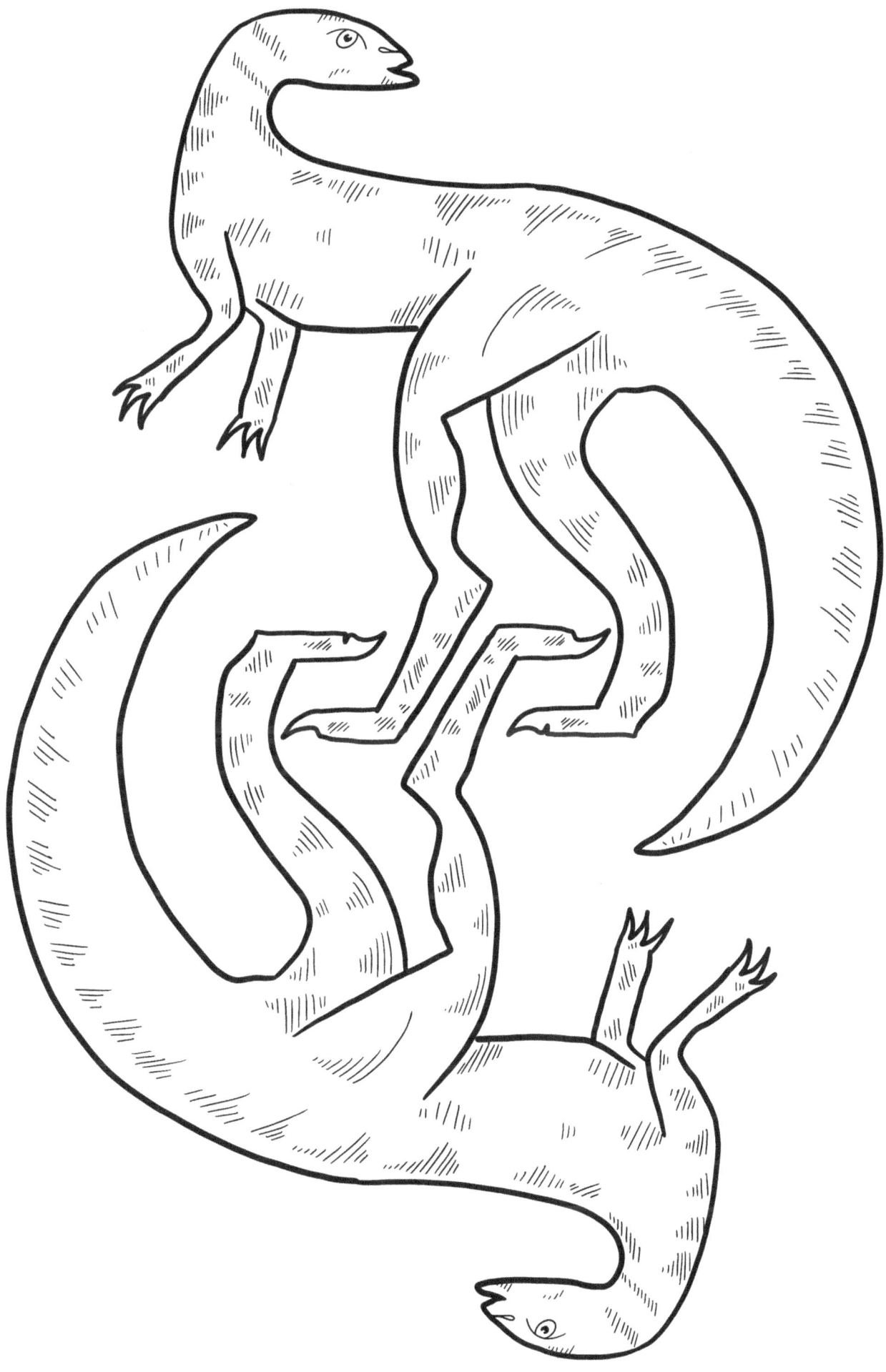

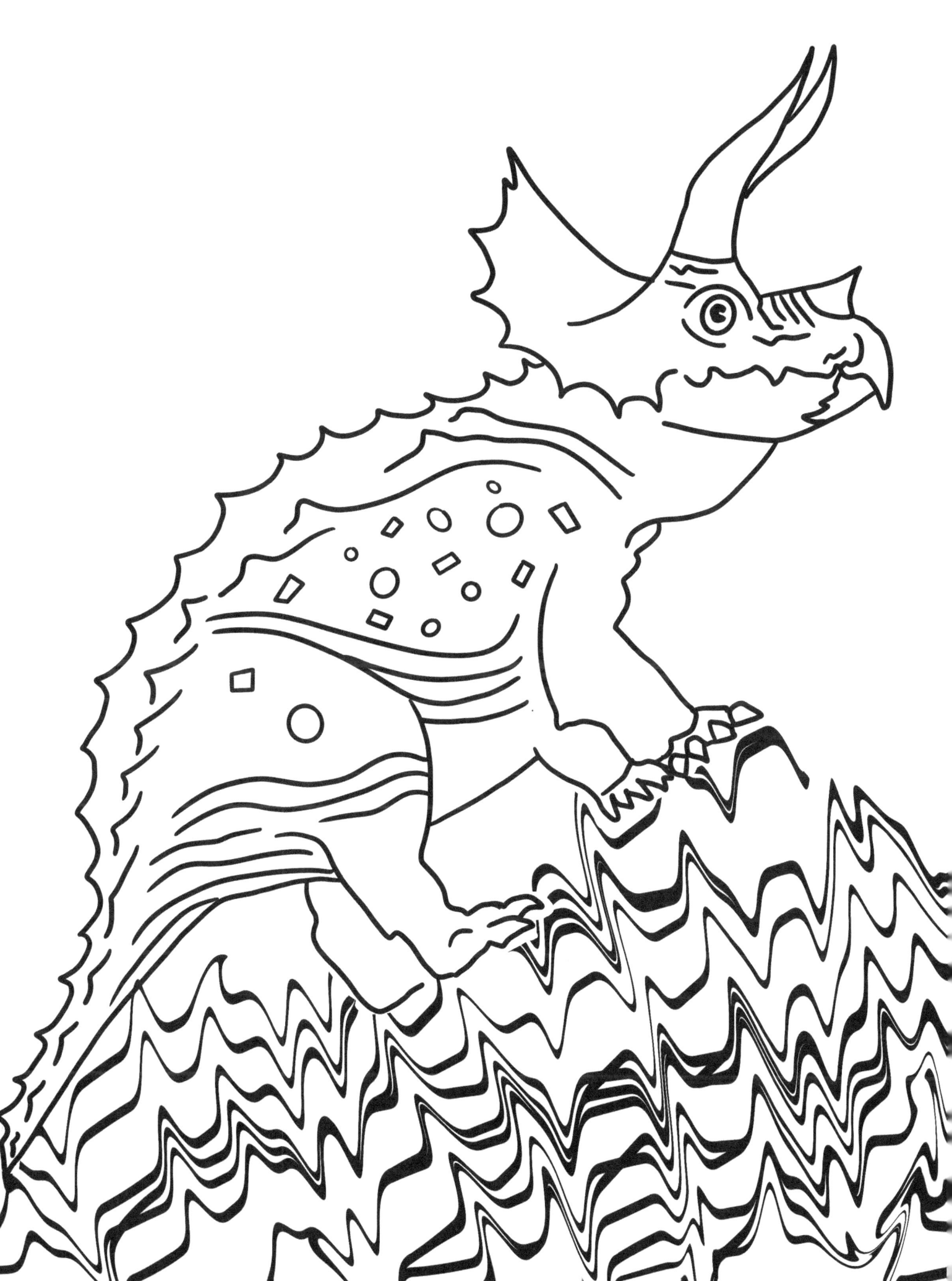

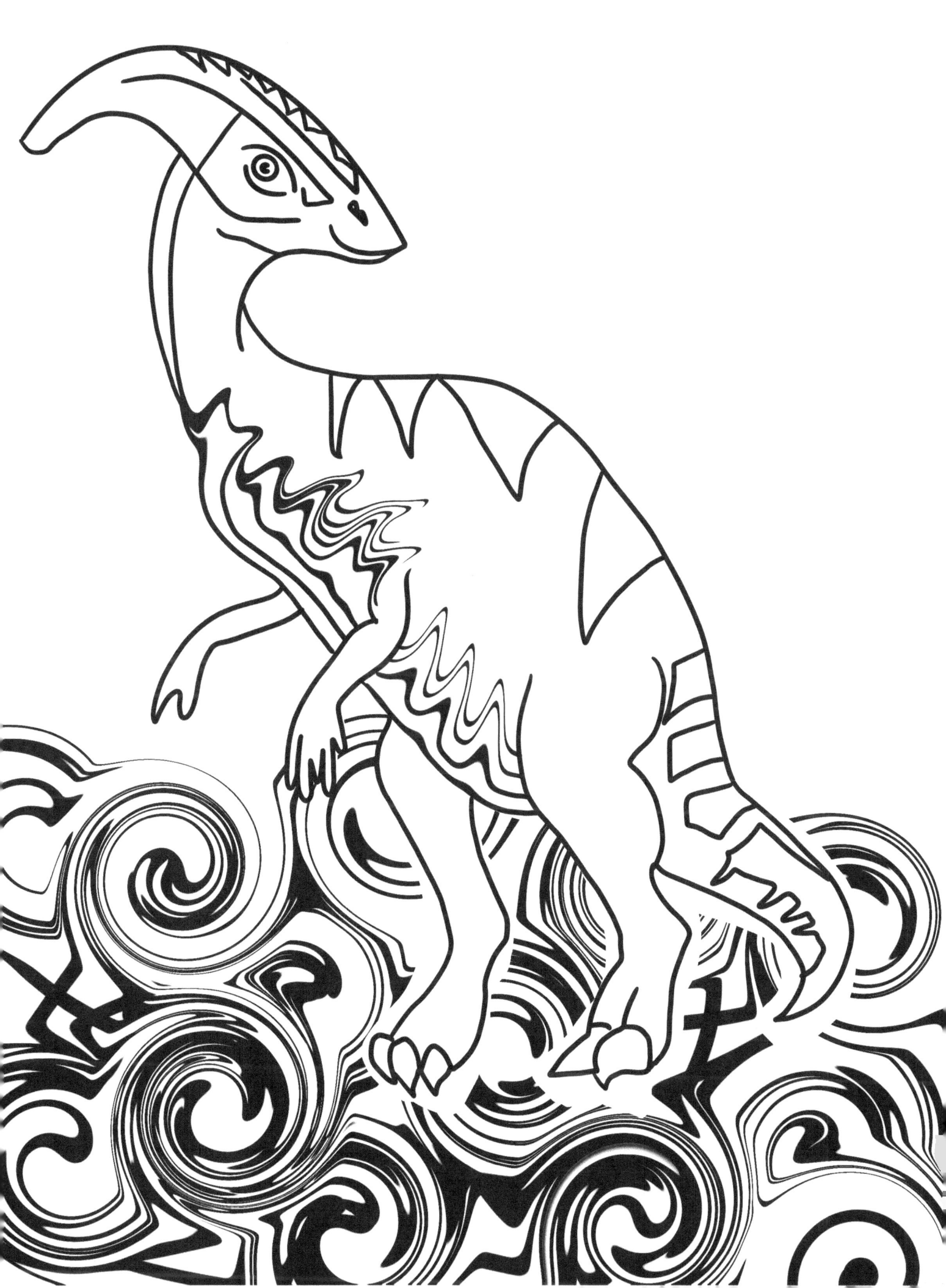

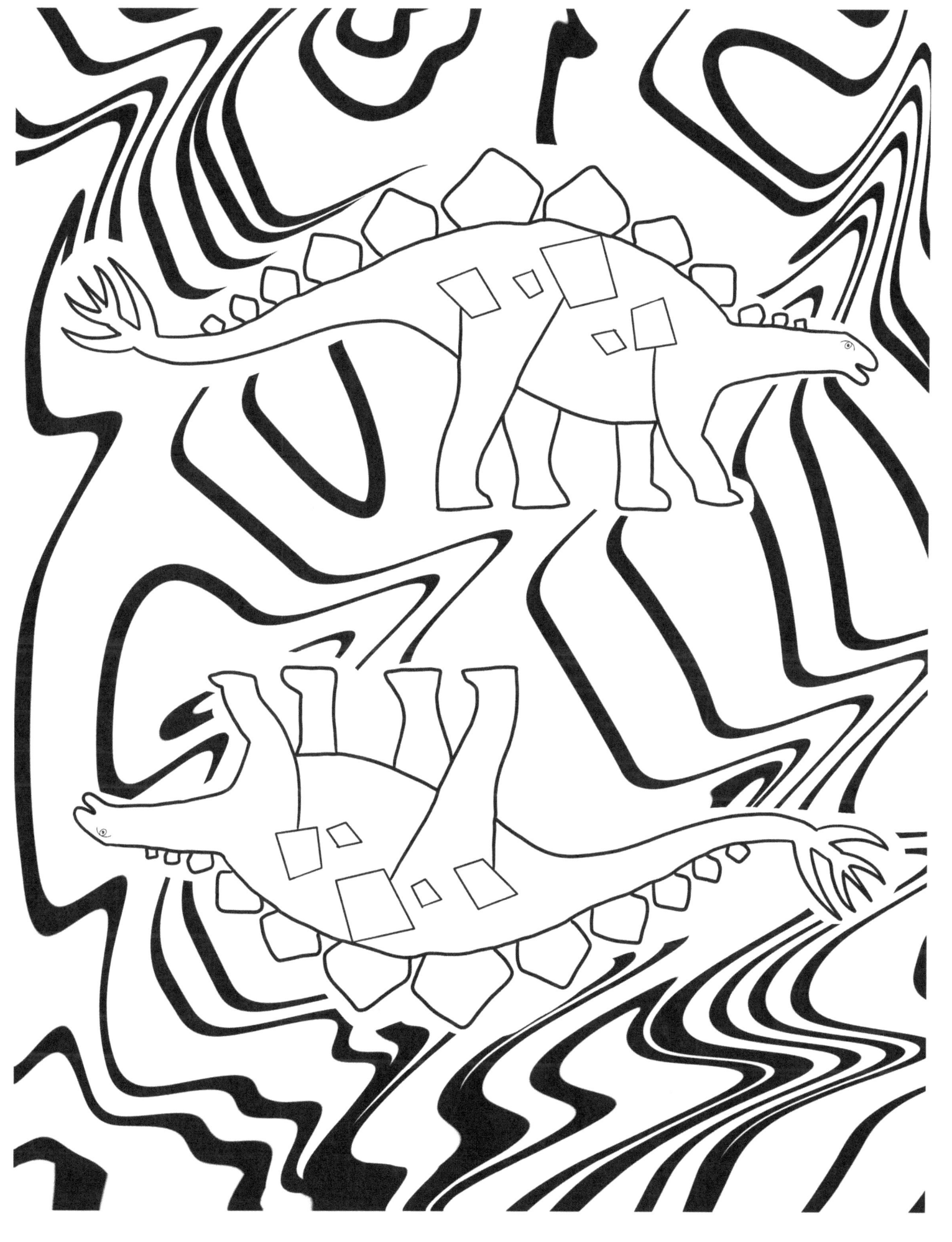

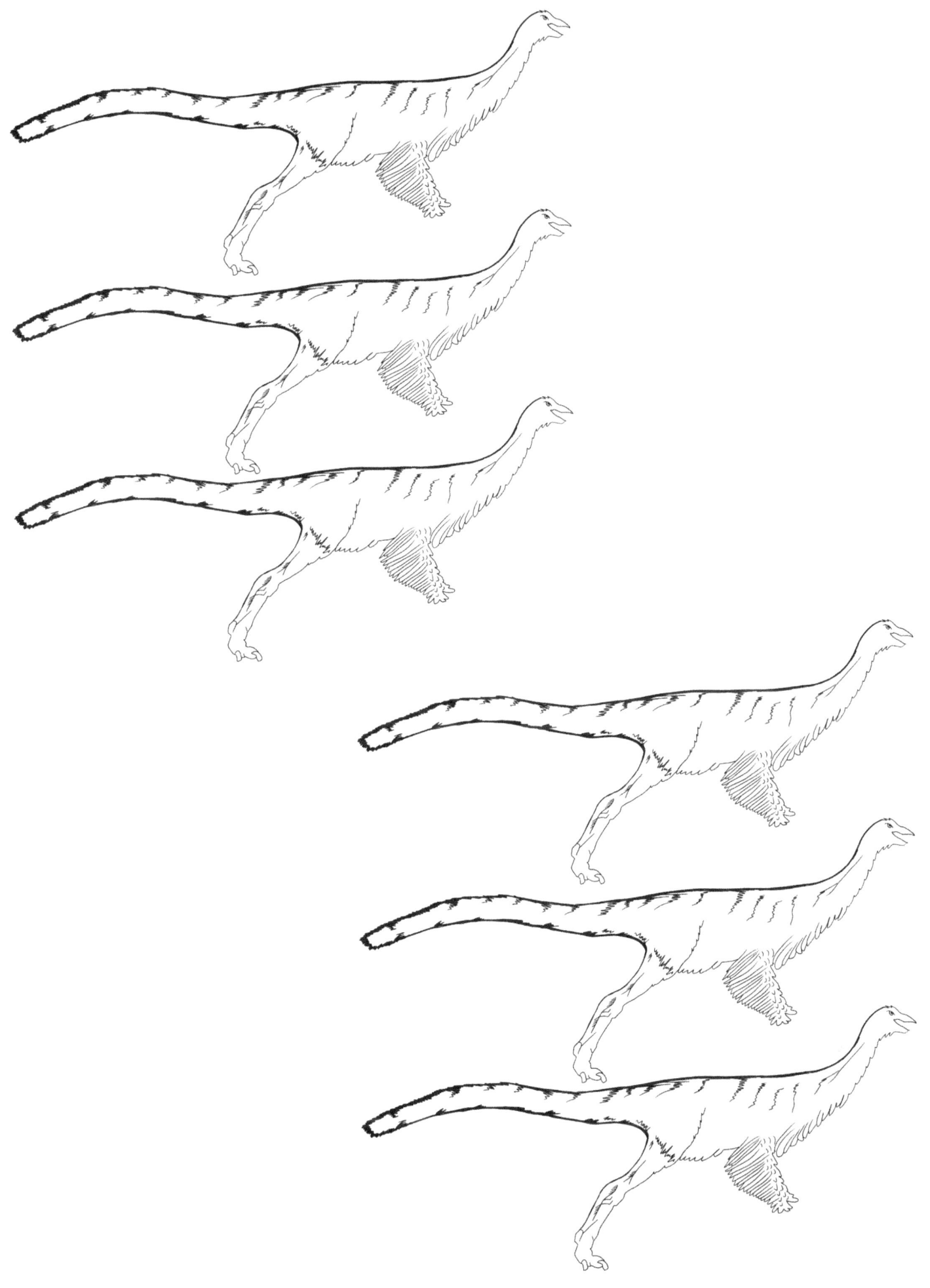

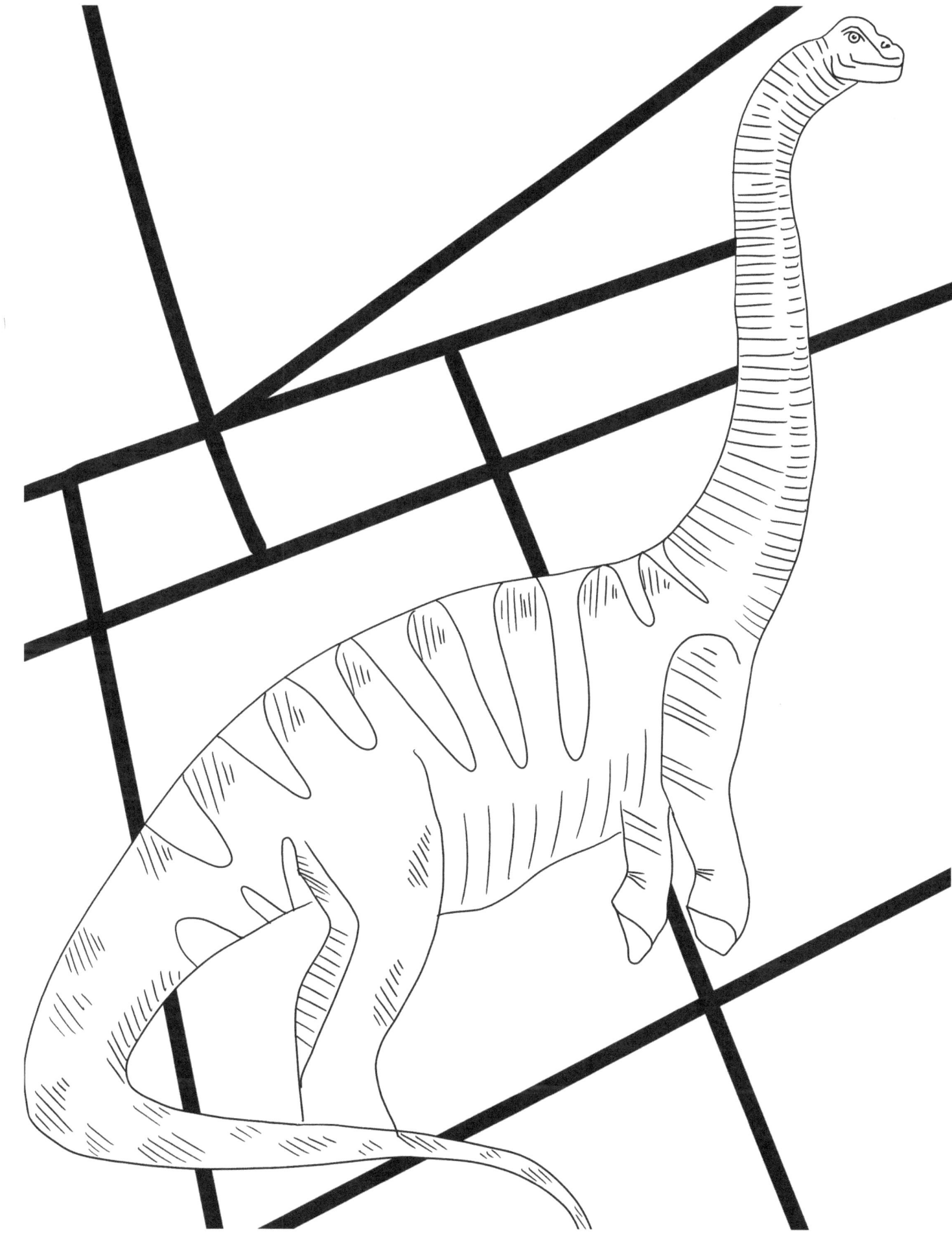

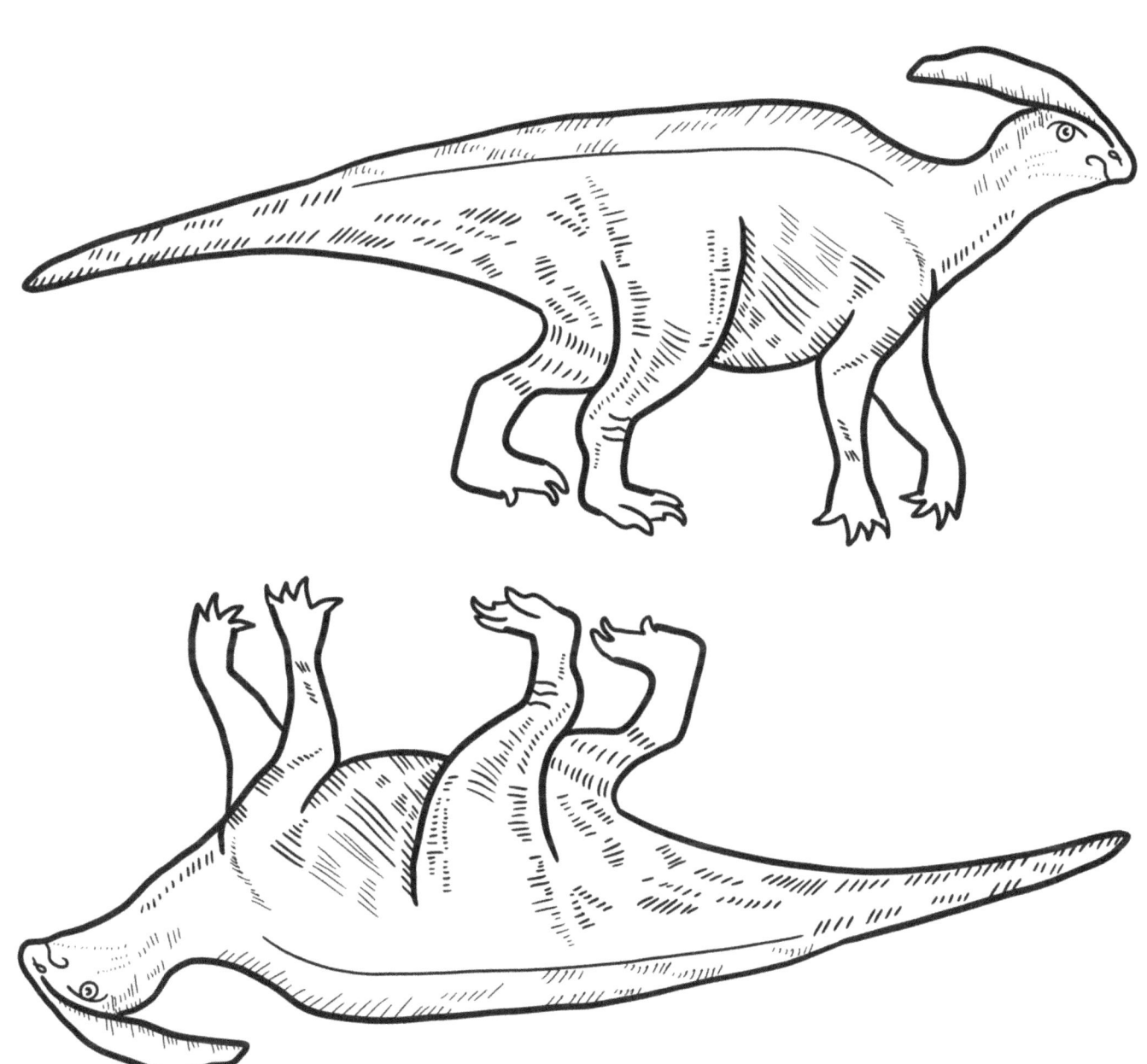

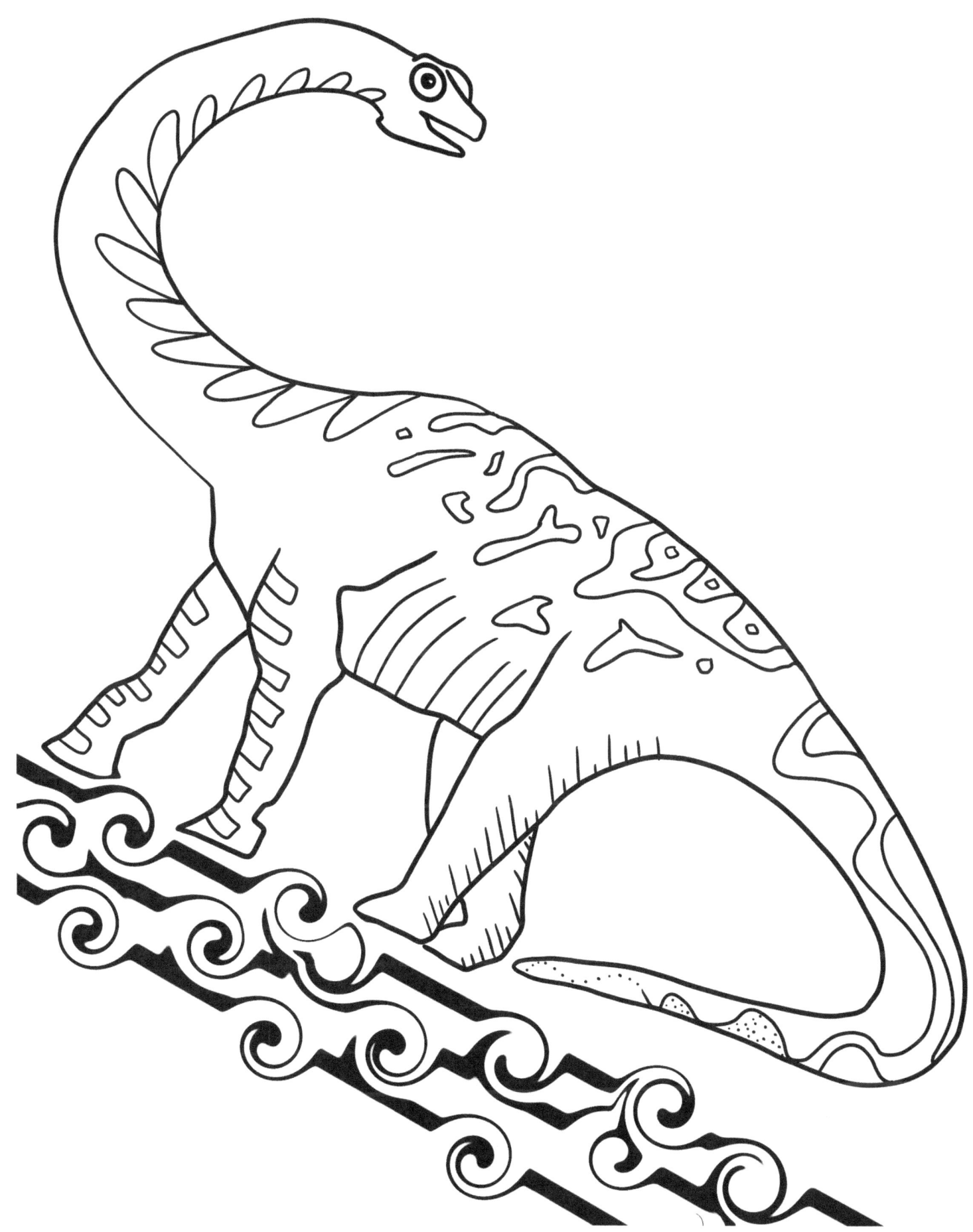

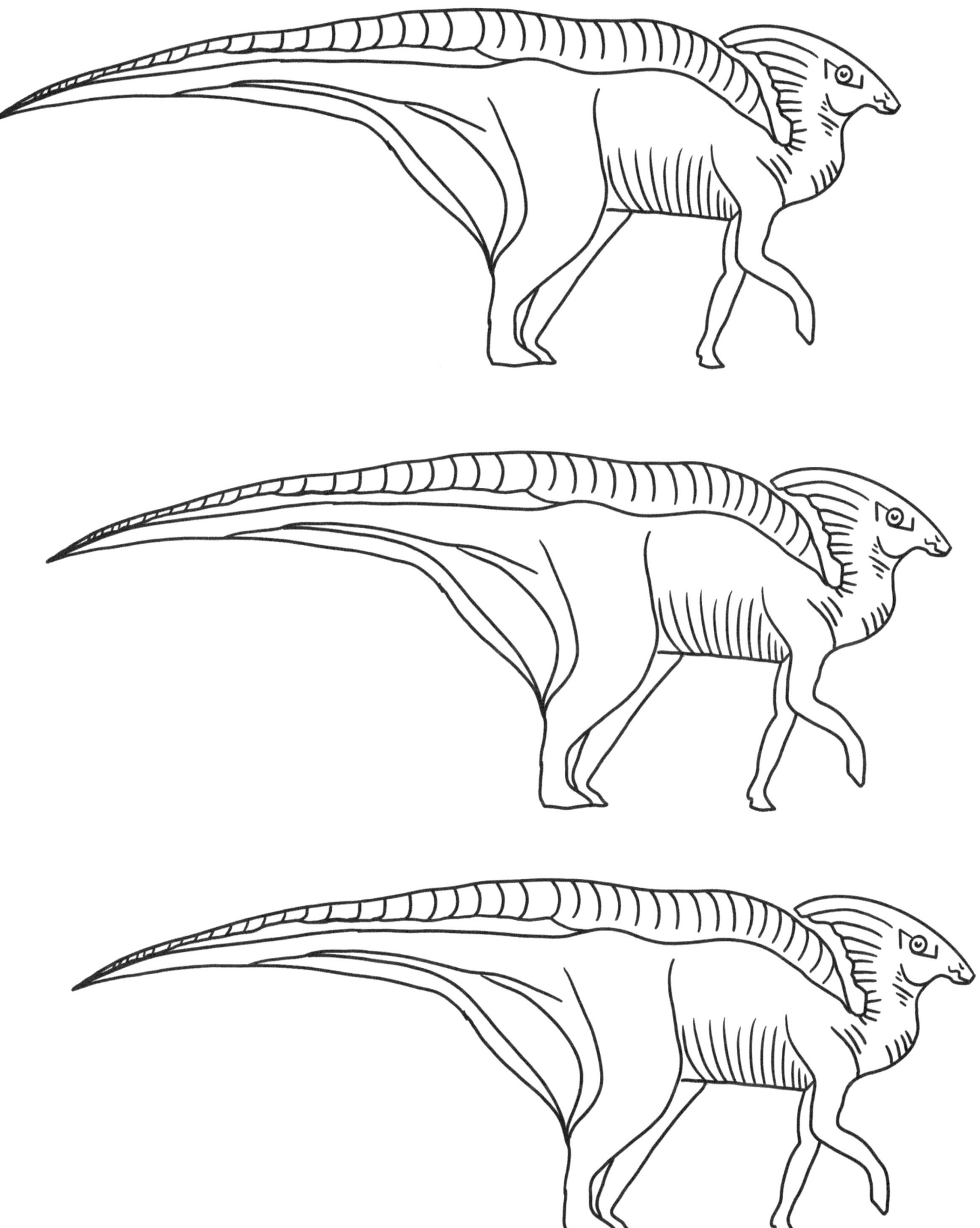

www.ingramcontent.com/pod-product-compliance
Lightning Source LLC
Chambersburg PA
CBHW081059240526
45465CB00025B/2761